M000202439

CAMBRIDGE'S CLASSIC GUIDE TO SUCCESS IN THE WORLD

MICROCOSMOGRAPHIA ACADEMICA

CAMBRIDGE'S CLASSIC
GUIDE TO
SUCCESS IN THE WORLD

MICROCOSMOGRAPHIA
ACADEMICA

BEING A GUIDE FOR THE YOUNG
ACADEMIC POLITICIAN

F. M. CORNFORD

MainSail Press
CAMBRIDGE

MainSail Press
in care of
QUEENS' COLLEGE
UNIVERSITY OF CAMBRIDGE
CAMBRIDGE CB3 9ET

US Office: MainSail Press,
944 Northwest 9th Court, Miami, Florida 33136

ISBN 0-9518684-1-1

First published by Bowes & Bowes, Cambridge, 1908
10th edition by MainSail Press, 1993
©1908, 1922, 1933, 1949, 1953, 1970 by Bowes & Bowes
©1993 Forward and Notes by MainSail Press

British Library Cataloguing in Publication Data
A catalogue record for this book
is available from the British Library

Printed in England by
St. Edmundsbury Press, Bury St. Edmunds
Bound and produced in Scotland by
Hunter & Foulis, Edinburgh

TABLE OF

CONTENTS

HENRY CHADWICK

FRANCIS Macdonald Cornford (1874-1943) was a Fellow of Trinity College Cambridge and became Cambridge's first professor of ancient philosophy. His books on Socrates, Plato, and Aristotle have often been reprinted and half a century after his death remain engrossing reading. He combined a powerful intelligence with delightful personal qualities, a special characteristic being his detachment from the opinions of established convention. By instinct an artist, musician, and poet, he married a poet—granddaughter of Charles Darwin. His mind always wanted to explore untrodden paths, to look at old problems from fresh angles, and to try to get beyond and behind his texts to discover the atmosphere of feeling in which their authors wrote. Like the historian of ancient Greek religion, Jane Harrison, who deeply influenced his standpoint (though he had far more respect than she for exactitude in scholarship), he sought to discover what the ancient authors really thought and felt. The son of a priest of the Church of England, he was profoundly sensitive to the non-Christian and the primitive in an author apparently so near to Christianity as was Plato. He was aware that words could be merely at the surface, and that the real driving motives of human beings are often more complex.

Experience of the tortuous paths pursued by academic bodies in reaching (or avoiding) a decision led him to write this famous satire, *Microcosmographia Academica*, in 1908—that is, when he was still in his early thirties. It is more than an occasional piece arising out of a particular context. Its immediate occasion and impetus are no longer recoverable except in the sense that here was a manifesto by a youngish academic disillusioned by ultra-conservatives who sought to avert all changes. Perhaps in his sixties he might have written a similar piece on ultra-progressives persuaded that all changes and innovations are inherently desirable values.

Cornford's shrewd observation enabled him to produce a witty satire transcending his time and place. He touched weaknesses universal in human nature.

May, 1993

W.K.C. GUTHRIE

WHEN *Microcosmographia Academica* was reprinted in 1922, Cornford himself wrote a short preface on the subject of its continued relevance after fourteen years and a war. (It is to this preface, by the way, that we owe the admirable definition of Propaganda as 'that branch of the art of lying which consists in very nearly deceiving your friends without quite deceiving your enemies.') It may be supposed that, had he lived, he would have added a few more words in explanation of its reappearance after another twenty-seven years and the upheaval of a second and greater war. If I may attempt to fill a gap which only he could have filled adequately, I would say first that the justification of *Microcosmographia* does not lie only in its relevance to the present situation. It is already a classic. The academic scene is indeed changed since 1908, but it is only an additional pleasure to come unexpectedly upon such historical details as the prohibition of walking to Madingley on Sundays without academical dress. I will not deprive the new reader of this pleasure by mentioning others. It seems perhaps more serious that whereas Cornford's enemy was inertia ('There is only one argument for doing something; the rest are arguments for doing nothing'), we may reasonably hold today that the greatest peril to the things which we value (and he valued) lies in too rapid change. Unfortunately too, we can no longer confine on the unregenerate Adullamites the description that they are 'dangerous,

because they know what they want; and
that is, all the money going.' Yet after all,
in so far as they are a menace, the changes
of today are for the most part not caused
by academics themselves. They tend to
originate outside, and is not the reason for
their success very largely the persistence
of the old arguments for doing nothing
about it among those who, given a few
more of the qualities of the Young Man in
a Hurry, might have saved the situation?

I started by affirming that the
appeal of *Microcosmographia* does not
depend on its continued relevance to the
current situation, but have drifted into
maintaining that relevance persists. This
I profoundly believe. No one who has
served on a College Governing Body or
Faculty Board can read without immediate recognition the chapters on Argument
and the Conduct of Business. Cornford
mentions the applicability of his principles
to government departments in the first

world war. I myself can vouch for the delight with which they were received in the second by those of my colleagues who seemed worthy to be introduced to them. Shortly before the war moreover I tried the book on the head of an electrical engineering firm, and he assured me that the business world itself was in urgent need of its counsel. Nor is it idle to mention that in 1945 the publishers received a request from the University of Chicago Press to print a small private edition to be given away to a select number of friends. The Argument of the Wedge, or the Principle of Unripe Time, cannot be out of date. They have roots in no changing historical situation, but in human nature. Read and see.

July, 1949

TO THE SECOND EDITION

THERE was a time towards the end of 1914, when many people imagined that after the war human nature, in our part of the world, would be different. They even thought it would be better in some ways. I have an idea that I shared in this illusion. But my friends who are still active in this microcosm tell me that academic human nature, at any rate, remains true to the ancient type. Moreover, a short and inglorious career in the home forces and in a Government department has convinced me that the academic species is only one member of a genus wider than I had supposed. Frequenters of the Church Congress, too, have admitted that they sometimes turn to the pages of this guide for help. Considering all this, I have persuaded the publishers to reprint it as it stands.

I fancy (though I am not sure) that there is not one feature of academic life that has become a little more prominent since the war. If I could have recaptured the mood of the fortnight in which this book was written, I might have added a chapter on Propaganda, defined as that branch of the art of lying which consists in very nearly deceiving your friends without quite deceiving your enemies. But the subject is not yet ripe for treatment; the art is still imperfect. We must leave it to be worked out by the party whose mission it is to keep the university safe for aristo-democracy.

F. M. C.

October, 1922

TO

EDWARD GRANVILLE BROWNE

ADVERTISEMENT

*IF YOU ARE YOUNG, do not read this book;
it is not fit for you;
IF YOU ARE OLD, throw it away;
you have nothing to learn from it;
IF YOU ARE UNAMBITIOUS, light the fire with it;
you do not need its guidance.*

*BUT, if you are neither less than twenty-five years old,
nor more than thirty,
AND if you are ambitious withal
and your spirit hankers after academic politics,
READ,
and may your soul (if you have one) find mercy!*

I *WARNING*

ANY ONE OF US might say, that although in words he is not able to meet you at each step of the argument, he sees as a fact that academic persons, when they carry out their study, not only in youth as a part of education, but as the pursuit of their maturer years, most of them become decidedly queer, not to say rotten; and that those who may be considered the best of them are made useless to the world by the very study which you extol.'

'Well, do you think that those who say so are wrong?'

'I cannot tell,' he replied, 'but I should like to know what is your opinion?'

'Hear my answer; I am of the opinion that they are quite right.'

PLATO, *Republic*, vi

MY heart is full of pity for you, O young academic politician. If you *will* be a politician you have a painful path to follow, even though it be a short one, before you nestle down into a modest incompetence. While you are young you will be oppressed, and angry, and increasingly disagreeable. When you reach middle age, at five-and-thirty, you will become complacent and, in your turn, an oppressor; those whom you oppress will find you still disagreeable; and so will all the people whose toes you trod upon in youth. It will seem to you then that you grow wiser every day, as you learn more and more of the reasons why things should not be done, and understand more fully the peculiarities of powerful persons, which make it quixotic even to attempt them without first going through an amount of squaring and lobbying sufficient to sicken any but the most hardened soul. If you persist to the threshold of old age—your fiftieth year, let us say—you will be a powerful person yourself, with an accretion of peculiarities which other people will have to study in order to square you. The toes you will have trodden on by this time will be as the sands of the seashore; and from far below you will mount the roar of a ruthless multitude of young men in a hurry. You may perhaps grow to be aware what they are in a hurry to do. They are in a hurry to get you out of the way.

O young academic politician, my heart is full of pity for you now; but when you are old, if you will stand in the way, there will be no more pity for you than you deserve; and that will be none at all.

I shall take it that you are in the first flush of ambition, and just beginning to make yourself disagreeable. You think (do you not?) that you have only to state a reasonable case, and people must listen to reason and act upon it at once. It is just this conviction that makes you so unpleasant. There is little hope of dissuading you; but has it occurred to you that nothing is ever done until everyone is convinced that it ought to be done, and has been convinced for so long that it is now time to do something else? And are you not aware that conviction has never yet been produced by an appeal to reason, which only makes people uncomfortable? If you want to move them, you must address your arguments to prejudice and the political motive, which I will presently describe. I should hesitate to write down so elementary a principle, if I were not sure you need to be told it. And you will not believe me, because you think your cases are so much more reasonable than mine can have been, and you are ashamed to study men's weaknesses and prejudices. You would rather batter away at the Shield of Faith than spy out the joints in the harness.

I like you the better for your illusions; but it cannot be denied that they prevent you from being effective, and if you do not become effective before you cease to want anything to be done—why, what will be the good of you? So I present you with this academic microcosmography—the merest sketch of the little world that lies before you. A satirist or an embittered man might have used darker colours; and I own that I have only drawn those aspects which it is most useful that you, as a politician, should know. There is another world within this microcosm—a silent, reasonable world, which you are now bent on leaving. Some day you may go back to it; and you will enjoy its calm the more for your excursion in the world of unreason.

Now listen, and I will tell you what this outer world is like.

II *PARTIES*

First, perhaps, I had better describe the parties in academic politics; not that it is easy to distinguish them precisely. There are five; and they are called Conservative Liberals, Liberal Conservatives, Non-placets, Adullamites and Young Men in a Hurry.

A *Conservative Liberal* is a broad-minded man, who thinks that something ought to be done, only not anything that anyone now desires, but something which was not done in 1881-82.

A *Liberal Conservative* is a broad-minded man, who thinks that something ought to be done, only not anything that anyone now desires; and most things which were done in 1881-82 ought to be undone.

The men of both of these parties are alike in being open to conviction; but so many convictions have already got inside, that it is very difficult to find the openings. They dwell in the Valley of Indecision.

The *Non-placet* differs in not being open to conviction; he is a man of principle.[1] A principle is a rule of inaction, which states a valid general reason for not doing in any particular case what, to an unprincipled instinct, would appear to be right. The Non-placet believes that it is always well to be on the Safe Side, which can easily be located on the northern side of the interior of the Senate House. He will be a person whom you have never seen before, and will never see again anywhere but in his favourite station on the left of the place of judgment.

The *Adullamites* are dangerous, because they know what they want; and that is, all the money there is going.[2] They inhabit a series of caves near Downing Street. They say to one another, 'If you scratch my back, I will scratch yours; and if you won't, I will scratch your face.' It will be seen that these cave-dwellers are not refined, like classical men. That is why they succeed in getting all the money there is going.

The *Young Man in a Hurry* is a narrow-minded and ridiculously youthful prig, who is inexperienced enough to imagine that something might be done before very long, and even to suggest definite things. His most dangerous defect being want of experience, everything should be done to prevent him from taking any part in affairs. He may be known by his propensity to organise societies for the purpose of making silk purses out of sows' ears. This tendency is not so dangerous as it might seem; for it may be observed that the sows, after taking their washing with a grunt or two, trundle back unharmed to the wallow; and the purse-market is quoted as firm. The Young Man in a Hurry is afflicted with a conscience, which is apt to break out, like measles, in patches. To listen to him, you would think that he united the virtues of a Brutus to the passion for lost causes of a Cato; he has not learnt that most of his causes are lost by letting the Cato out of the bag, instead of tying him up firmly and sitting on him, as experienced people do.

O young academic politician, know thyself!

III *CAUCUSES*

A CAUCUS is like a mouse trap; when you are outside you want to get in; and when you are inside the mere sight of the other mice makes you want to get out. The trap is baited with muffins and cigars—except in the case of the Non-placet caucus, an ascetic body, which, as will presently be seen, satisfies only spiritual needs.

The *Adullamites* hold a Caucus from time to time to conspire against the College System. They wear blue spectacles and false beards, and say the most awful things to one another. There are two ways of dispersing these anarchs.

One is to suggest that working hours might be lengthened. The other is to convert the provider of muffins and cigars to Conservative Liberalism. To mention belling the cat would be simply indecent.[3]

No one can tell the difference between a *Liberal Conservative* Caucus and a *Conservative Liberal* one. There is nothing in the world more innocent than either. The most dare-devil action they ever take is to move for the appointment of a Syndicate 'to consider what means, if any, can be discovered to prevent the Public Washing of Linen, and to report, if they can see straight, to the Non-placets.' The result is the formation of an invertebrate body, which sits for two years, with growing discomfort, on the clothes-basket containing the linen. When the Syndicate is so stupefied that it has quite forgotten what it is sitting on, it issues three minority reports, of enormous bulk, on some different subject. The reports are referred by the Council to the Non-placets, and by the Non-placets to the wastepaper basket. This is called 'reforming the University from within.'

At election time each of these two Caucuses meets to select for nomination those members of its own party who are most likely to be mistaken by the Non-placets for members of the other party. The best results are achieved when the nominees get mixed up in such a way that the acutest of Non-placets cannot divine which ticket represents which party. The system secures that the balance of power shall be most happily maintained, and that all the Young Men in a Hurry shall be excluded.

The *Young Men in a Hurry* have no regular Caucus. They meet, by twos and threes, in desolate places, and gnash their teeth.

The *Non-placet* Caucus exists for

the purpose of distributing Church patronage among those of its members who have adhered immovably to the principles of the party.

All Caucuses have the following rule. At Caucus meetings which are only attended by one member (owing to that member's having omitted to summon the others), the said member shall be deemed to constitute a quorum, and may vote the meeting full powers to go on the square without further ceremony.[4]

IV *ON ACQUIRING INFLUENCE*

Now that you know about the Parties and the Caucuses, your first business will be to acquire influence. Political influence may be acquired in exactly the same way as the gout; indeed, the two ends ought to be pursued concurrently. The method is to sit tight and drink port wine. You will thus gain the reputation of being a good fellow; and not a few wild oats will be condoned in one who is sound at heart, if not at the lower extremities.

Or perhaps, you may prefer to qualify as a *Good Business Man*.

He is one whose mind has not

been warped and narrowed by merely intellectual interests, and who, at the same time, has not those odious pushing qualities which are unhappily required for making a figure in business anywhere else. He has had his finger on the pulse of the Great World— a distant and rather terrifying region, which it is very necessary to keep in touch with, though it must not be allowed on any account to touch you. Difficult as it seems, this relation is successfully maintained by sending young men to the Bar with Fellowships of £200 a year and no duties. Life at the Bar, in these conditions, is very pleasant; and only good business men are likely to return.[5] All business men are good; and it is understood that they let who will, be clever: provided he be not clever at their expense.

V *THE PRINCIPLES OF GOVERNMENT,*
OF DISCIPLINE (INCLUDING RELIGION)
AND OF SOUND LEARNING

THESE principles are all deducible from the fundamental maxim, that the first necessity for a body of men engaged in the pursuit of learning is freedom from the burden of political cares. It is impossible to enjoy the contemplation of truth if one is vexed and distracted by the sense of responsibility. Hence the wisdom of our ancestors devised a form of academic polity in which this sense is, so far as human imperfection will allow, reduced to the lowest degree. By vesting the sovereign authority in the Non-placets (technically known as the ' Senate ' on account of the high average of their age), our fore-fathers secured that the final decision should rest with a body which, being scattered in country parsonages, has no corporate feeling whatever,[6] and, being necessarily ignorant of the decisive considerations in almost all the business submitted to it, cannot have the sense of any responsibility, except it be the highest, when the Church is in danger. In the smaller bodies, called 'Boards,' we have succeeded only in minimising the dangerous feeling, by the means of never allowing anyone to act without first consulting at least twenty other people who are accustomed to regard him with well-founded suspicion. Other democracies have reached this pitch of excellence; but the academic democracy is superior in having no organised parties. We thus avoid all the responsibilities of party leadership (there are leaders, but no one follows them), and the degradations of party compromise. It is clear, moreover, that twenty independent persons, each of whom has a different reason for not doing a certain thing, and no one of whom will compromise with any other, constitute a most effective check upon the rashness of individuals.

I forgot to mention that there is also a body called the 'Council,' which consists of men who are firmly convinced that they are business-like. There is no doubt that some of them are Good Business Men.

The principle of Discipline (including Religion) is that *there must be some rules.* If you inquire the reason, you will find that the object of rules is to relieve the younger men of the burdensome feeling of moral or religious obligation. If their energies are to be left unimpaired for the pursuit of athletics, it is clearly necessary to protect them against the weakness of their own characters. They must never be troubled with having to think whether this or that ought to be done or not; it should be settled by rules. The most valuable rules are those which ordain attendance at lectures and at religious worship. If these were not enforced, young men would begin too early to take learning and religion seriously; and that is well known to be bad form. Plainly, the more rules you can invent, the less need there will be to waste time over fruitless puzzling about right and wrong. The best sort of rules are those which prohibit important, but perfectly innocent, actions, such as smoking in College Courts, or walking to Madingley on Sunday without academical dress. The merit of such regulations is that, having nothing to do with right or wrong, they help to obscure these troublesome considerations in other cases, and to relieve the mind of all sense of obligation towards society.

The Roman sword would never have conquered the world if the grand fabric of Roman Law had not been elaborated to save the man behind the sword from having to think for himself. In the same way the British Empire is the outcome of College and School discipline and of the Church Catechism.

The Principle of Sound Learning is that the noise of vulgar fame should never trouble the cloistered calm of academic existence. Hence, learning is called sound when no one has ever heard of it; and 'sound scholar' is a term of praise applied to one another by learned men who have no reputation outside the University, and a rather queer one inside it. If you should write a book (you had better not), be sure that it is unreadable; otherwise you will be called 'brilliant' and forfeit all respect.[7]

University printing presses exist, and are subsidised by the Government, for the purpose of producing books which no one can read; and they are true to their high calling. Books are the sources of material for lectures. They should be kept from the young; for to read books and remember what you read, well enough to reproduce it, is called 'cramming,' and this is destructive of all true education. The best way to protect the young from books is, first, to make sure that they shall be so dry as to offer no temptation; and, second, to store them in such a way that no one can find them without several years' training. A lecturer is a sound scholar, who is chosen to teach on the ground that he was once able to learn. Eloquence is not permissible in a lecturer; it is a privilege reserved by statute for the Public Orator.[8]

VI *THE POLITICAL MOTIVE*

You will begin, I suppose, by thinking that people who disagree with you and oppress you must be dishonest. Cynicism is the besetting and venial fault of declining youth, and disillusionment its last illusion. It is quite a mistake to suppose that real dishonesty is at all common. The number of rogues is about equal to the number of men who act honestly; and it is very small. The great majority would sooner behave honestly than not. The reason why they do not give way to this natural preference of humanity is that they are afraid that others will not; and the others do not because they are afraid that *they* will not. Thus it comes about that, while behaviour which looks dishonest is fairly common, sincere dishonesty is about as rare as the courage to evoke good faith in your neighbours by showing that you trust them.

No; the Political Motive in the academic breast is honest enough. It is *Fear*—genuine, perpetual, heart-felt timorousness. We shall see presently that all the Political Arguments are addressed to this passion. Have you ever noticed how people say 'I'm *afraid* I don't . . .' when they mean, 'I *think* I don't . . .'?

The proper objects of Fear, hereafter to be called *Bugbears*, are (in order of importance):

Giving yourself away;
Females;
What Dr—— will say;
The Public Washing of Linen;
Socialism, otherwise Atheism;
The Great World; etc. etc. etc.

With the disclosure of this central mystery of academic politics, the theoretical part of our treatise is complete. The practical principles, to which we now turn, can nearly all be deduced from the nature of the political passion and of its objects.

The Practice of Politics may be divided under three heads: *Argument*, *The Conduct of Business*, *Squaring*.

VII *ARGUMENT*

THERE is only one argument
for doing something; the rest are arguments for doing nothing.

The argument for doing some-
thing is that it is the right thing to do. But
then, of course, comes the difficulty of
making sure that it is right. Females act
by mere instinctive intuition; but men
have the gift of reflection. As Hamlet, the
typical man of action, says:

> What is a man,
> If his chief good and market of his time
> Be but to sleep and feed? a beast, no more.
> Sure, he that made us with such large discourse,
> Looking before and after, gave us not
> That capability and god-like reason
> To fust in us unused.

Now the academic person is to Hamlet as Hamlet is to a female; or, to use his own quaint phrase, a 'beast'; his discourse is many times larger, and he looks before and after many times as far. Even a little knowledge of ethical theory will suffice to convince you that all important questions are so complicated, and the results of any course of action are so difficult to foresee, that certainty, or even probability, is seldom, if ever, attainable. It follows at once that the only justifiable attitude of mind is suspense of judgment; and this attitude, besides being peculiarly congenial to the academic temperament, has the advantage of being comparatively easy to attain. There remains the duty of persuading others to be equally judicious, and to refrain from plunging into reckless courses which might lead them Heaven knows whither. At this point the arguments for doing nothing come in; for it is a mere theorist's paradox that doing nothing has just as many consequences as doing something. It is obvious that inaction can have no consequences at all.

Since the stone-axe fell into disuse at the close of the neolithic age, two other arguments of universal application have been added to the rhetorical armoury by the ingenuity of mankind. They are closely akin; and, like the stone-axe, they are addressed to the Political Motive. They are called the *Wedge* and the *Dangerous Precedent*. Though they are very familiar, the principles, or rules of inaction, involved in them are seldom stated in full. They are as follows.

The *Principle of the Wedge* is that you should not act justly now for fear of raising expectations which you are afraid you will not have the courage to satisfy. A little reflection will make it evident that the Wedge argument implies the admission that the persons who use it cannot prove that the action is not just. If they

could, that would be the sole and sufficient reason for not doing it, and this
argument would be superfluous.

The *Principle of the Dangerous
Precedent* is that you should not now do an
admittedly right action for fear you, or
your equally timid successors, should not
have the courage to do right in some
future case, which, *ex hypothesi*, is essen-
tially different, but superficially resembles
the present one. Every public action
which is not customary, either is wrong,
or, if it is right, is a dangerous precedent.
It follows that nothing should ever be
done for the first time.

It will be seen that both the Political Arguments are addressed to the Bugbear of *Giving yourself away*. Other special
arguments can be framed in view of the
other Bugbears. It will often be sufficient
to argue that a change is a change—an
irrefutable truth. If this consideration is
not decisive, it may be reinforced by the

Fair Trial Argument—'*Give the present system a Fair Trial.*' This is especially useful in withstanding changes in the schedule of an examination. In this connection the exact meaning of the phrase is, 'I don't intend to alter my lectures if I can help it; and, if you pass this proposal, you will have to alter yours.' This paraphrase explains what might otherwise be obscure: namely, the reason why a Fair Trial ought only to be given to systems which already exist, not to proposed alternatives.

Another argument is that '*the Time is not Ripe.*' The Principle of Unripe Time is that people should not do at the present moment what they think right at that moment, because the moment at which they think it right has not yet arrived. But the unripeness of the time will, in some cases, be found to lie in the Bugbear, 'What Dr— will say.' Time, by the way, is like the medlar; it has a trick of going rotten before it is ripe.

VIII   *THE CONDUCT OF BUSINESS*

THIS naturally divides into two branches; (1) *Conservative Liberal Obstruction*, and (2) *Liberal Conservative Obstruction*.

The former is by much the more effective; and should always be preferred to mere unreasonable opposition, because it will bring you the reputation of being more advanced than any so-called reformer.

The following are the main types of argument suitable for the *Conservative Liberal*.

'*The present measure would block the way for a far more sweeping reform.*' The reform in question ought always to be one which was favoured by a few extremists in 1881, and which by this time is quite impracticable and not even desired by any one. This argument may safely be combined with the Wedge argument: 'If we grant this, it will be impossible to stop short.' It is a singular fact that all measures are always opposed on both these grounds. The apparent discrepancy is happily reconciled when it comes to voting.

Another argument is that *'the machinery for effecting the proposed objects already exists.'* This should be urged in cases where the existing machinery has never worked, and is now so rusty that there is no chance of its being set in motion. When this is ascertained, it is safe to add that *'it is far better that all reform should come from within'*; and to throw in a reference to the *Principle of Washing Linen*. This principle is that it is better never to wash your linen if you cannot do it without anyone knowing that you are so cleanly.[9]

The third accepted means of obstruction is the *Alternative Proposal*. This is a form of Red Herring. As soon as three or more alternatives are in the field, there is pretty sure to be a majority against any one of them, and nothing will be done.

The method of *Prevarication* is based upon a very characteristic trait of the academic mind, which comes out in the common remark, 'I was in favour of the proposal until I heard Mr—'s argument in support of it.' The principle is, that a few bad reasons for doing something neutralise all the good reasons for doing it. Since this is devoutly believed, it is often the best policy to argue weakly against the side you favour. If your personal enemies are present in force, throw in a little bear-baiting, and you are certain of success. You can vote in the minority, and no one will be the wiser.

Liberal Conservative Obstruction is less argumentative and leans to invective. It is particularly fond of the Last Ditch and the Wild Cat.

The *Last Ditch* is the Safe Side,[10] considered as a place which you may safely threaten to die in. You are not likely to die there prematurely; for, to judge by the look of the inhabitants, the climate of the Safe Side conduces to longevity. If you did die, nobody would much mind; but the threat may frighten them for the moment.

'*Wild Cat*' is an epithet applicable to persons who bring forward a scheme unanimously agreed upon by experts after two years' exhaustive consideration of thirty-five or more alternative proposals. In its wider use it applies to all ideas which were not familiar in 1881.

There is an oracle of Merlin which

says, 'When the wild cat is belled, the mice will vote *Placet.*'

The argument, '*that you remember exactly the same proposal being rejected in 1867,*' is a very strong one in itself; but its defect is that it appeals only to those who also remember the year 1867 with affectionate interest, and, moreover, are unaware that any change has occurred since then. There are such people, but they are lamentably few; and some even of them are no longer Young Men in a Hurry, and can be trusted to be on the Safe Side in any case. So this argument seldom carries its proper weight.

When other methods of obstruction fail, you should have recourse to *Wasting Time*; for, although it is recognised in academic circles that time in general is of no value, considerable importance is attached to teatime, and by deferring this, you may exasperate any body of men to the point of voting against anything. The simplest method is *Boring*. Talk slowly and indistinctly, at a little distance from the point. No academic person is ever voted into the chair until he has reached an age at which he has forgotten the meaning of the word 'irrelevant'; and you will be allowed to go on, until everyone in the room will vote with you sooner than hear your voice another minute. Then you should move for adjournment. Motions for adjournment, made less than fifteen minutes before teatime or at any subsequent moment, are always carried. While you are engaged in Boring it does not matter much what you talk about; but, if possible, you should discourse upon the proper way of doing something which you are notorious for doing badly yourself. Thus, if you are an inefficient lecturer, you should lay down the law on how to lecture; if you are a good business man, you should discuss the principles of finance and so on.

If you have applied yourself in youth to the cultivation of the *Private Business habit of mind* at the Union and other debating societies, questions of procedure will furnish you with many resources for wasting time. You will eagerly debate whether it is allowable or not to amend an amendment; or whether it is consonant with the eternal laws for a body of men, who have all changed their minds, to rescind a resolution which they have just carried. You will rise, like a fish, to points of order, and call your intimate friends 'honourable' to their faces. You will make six words do duty for one; address a harmless individual as if he were a roomful of abnormally stupid reporters; and fill up the time till you can think of something to say by talking, instead of by holding your tongue.

An appeal should be made, wherever it is possible, to *College Feeling*. This, like other species of patriotism, consists in a sincere belief that the institution to which you belong is better than an institution to which other people belong. The corresponding belief ought to be encouraged in others by frequent confession of this article of faith in their presence. In this way a healthy spirit of rivalry will be promoted. It is this feeling which makes the College System so valuable; and differentiates, more than anything else, a College from a boarding-house; for in a boarding-house hatred is concentrated, not upon rival establishments, but upon the other members of the same establishment.

Should you have a taste for winter sports, you may amuse yourself with a little *Bear-baiting* or *Bull-fighting*. Bulls are easier to draw than bears; you need only get to know the right red flag for a given bull, and for many of them almost any rag will serve the turn. Bears are more sulky and have to be prodded; on the other hand they don't go blind, like bulls; and when they have bitten your head off, they will often come round and be quite nice. Irishmen can be bulls, but not bears; Scotsmen can be bears, but not bulls; an Englishman may be either.

Another sport which wastes unlimited time is *Comma-hunting*. Once start a comma and the whole pack will be off, full cry, especially if they have had a literary training. (Adullamites affect to despise commas, and even their respect for syntax is often not above suspicion.) But comma-hunting is so exciting as to be a little dangerous. When attention is entirely concentrated on punctuation, there is some fear that the conduct of business may suffer, and a proposal get through without being properly obstructed on its demerits. It is therefore wise, when a kill has been made, to move at once for adjournment.

IX *SQUARING*

THIS most important branch of political activity is, of course, closely connected with *Jobs*.[11] These fall into two classes, My Jobs and Your Jobs. My Jobs are public-spirited proposals, which happen (much to my regret) to involve the advancement of a personal friend, or (still more to my regret) of myself. Your Jobs are insidious intrigues for the advancement of yourself and your friends, speciously disguised as public-spirited proposals. The term Job is more commonly applied to the second class. When you and I have, each of us, a Job on hand, we shall proceed to go on the Square.

Squaring can be carried on at lunch; but it is better that we would meet casually. The proper course to pursue is to walk, between 2 and 4 p.m., up and down the King's Parade, and more particularly that part of it which lies between the Colleges of Pembroke and Caius.[12] When we have succeeded in meeting accidentally, it is etiquette to talk about indifferent matters for ten minutes and then part. After walking five paces in the opposite direction you should call me back, and begin with the words, 'Oh, by the way, if you would happen . . .' The nature of Your Job must then be vaguely indicated, without mentioning names; and it should be treated by both parties as a matter of very small importance. You should hint that I am a very influential person, and that the whole thing is a secret between us. Then we shall part as before, and I shall call you back and introduce the subject of My Job, in the same formula. By observing this procedure we shall emphasise the fact that there is *no connection whatever* between my supporting your Job and your supporting mine. This absence of connection is the essential feature of Squaring.[13]

Remember this: *the men who get things done are the men who walk up and down King's Parade, from 2 to 4, every day of their lives.* You can either join them, and become a powerful person; or you can join the great throng of those who spend all their time in preventing them from getting things done, and in the larger task of preventing one another from doing anything whatever. This is the Choice of Hercules, when Hercules takes to politics.

X *FAREWELL*

O YOUNG academic politician, my heart is full of pity for you, because you will not believe a word that I have said. You will mistake sincerity for cynicism, and half the truth for exaggeration. You will think the other half of the truth, which I have not told, is the whole. You will take your own way, make yourself dreadfully disagreeable, tread on innumerable toes, butt your head against stone walls, neglect prejudice and fear, appeal to reason instead of appealing to bugbears. Your bread shall be bitterness, and your drink tears.

I have done what I could to warn

you. When you become middle-aged—
on your five-and-thirtieth birthday—
glance through this book and judge
between me and your present self.

If you decide that I was wrong, put
the book in the fire, betake yourself to the
King's Parade, and good-bye. I have done
with you.

But if you find that I was right,
remember that other world, within the
microcosm, the silent, reasonable world,
where the only action is thought, and
thought is free from fear. If you go back
to it now, keeping just enough bitterness
to put a pleasant edge on your conversation, and just enough worldly wisdom to
save other people's toes, you will find
yourself in the best of all company—the
company of clean, humorous intellect;
and if you have a spark of imagination and
try very hard to remember what it was like
to be young, there is no reason why your
brains should ever get woolly, or anyone

should wish you out of the way. Farewell!

EXPLICIT

1. *Non placet* (it is not pleasing) is the 'nay' in Senate House votes. As a widespread reactionary party, the *Non-placets* oppose all reforms. In a debate the *Non placet* side of the Senate House is along the north, to the left of the presiding chair, while the *Placet* side is along the south.

2. Adullamites are an alarming kind of reformers, named after David's band of rough conspirators who hid in desert caves at a place called Adullam (1 Samuel 22,1-2). Cornford's cave-dwellers were the scientists who inhabited extensive stone-fronted laboratory buildings then going up near Downing Street. They wanted to break the existing power of the colleges and had managed to attract their own outside funding for these large construction projects. Although much of the *Microcosmographia* scorns the old fogey who blocks reform, the Adullamites represent the wrong sort of progressive. Their uncivilised perversion of squaring, for instance, is to talk openly about scratching one another's backs and blatantly

threaten to attack anyone who will not support them.

3. If their cigars and muffins were denied them, they would lack incentive to meet. It would be uncivilised to suggest they were cowards for not putting their conspiratorial grumblings into bold action.

4. Squaring is explained on page 39.

5. College fellows embarking on legal careers in London depended on their fellowships to see them through the difficult initial years until they could attract briefs of their own. If they could not quite succeed at the Bar, they returned to the University, at least knowing their way around in the outside world. This is the good of them.

6. All holders of Master of Art status, that is, virtually all graduates of the University of more than five years' standing, belonged to the Senate and had a vote. Because the University had once been a chief source of clergymen, many graduates did indeed go to small parishes all over Britain. But Cambridge was thoroughly secularised by the time Cornford wrote, and the image of rustic country

parsons flocking back to Cambridge to swing a vote was a ridiculous stereotype of very old fogeys, and an example of responsibility being dispersed into thin air.

7. Making a popular name for oneself was frowned upon among the dons. That is one of the reasons why Cornford first published his *Microcosmographia* anonymously. Even after his identity as the author was found out, and admitted in the second edition, he still spoofed this donnish prejudice in an inscription in his own hand that appears in a rare 1923 American edition held by the University Library: *'from the anonymous and possibly (who knows?) pseudonymous Author.'*

8. The Public Orator is a University officer charged with composing and delivering speeches in Latin for august occasions.

9. This obstruction insists that keeping up a false appearance is superior to being overly attentive to cleanness.

10. The Safe Side is where the *Non-placets* reject all reforming graces. See page 7.

11. A Job is anything you want to get done, any project.

12. Exercise for many fellows consisted of long afternoon walks, which might well be turned to political purpose. Cornford jokes that they take long walks over a short distance.

13. Squaring, or going on the square, is making contact with an influential person—one who habitually takes an interest in an area your project touches upon. He is squared when he will not oppose you.

ACKNOWLEDGEMENTS

THE PUBLISHERS wish to thank Professor Christopher N. L. Brooke, the Dixie Professor of History at the University of Cambridge, who has given invaluable insights into the *Microcosmographia Academica*. Much of our conversation and mutual amusement could not find its way into these brief notes, but his most recent book, *A History of the University of Cambridge, Volume 4, 1870-1990* (CUP, 1993), elegantly and incisively describes the setting in which Cornford wrote.